WIDE RULED
COMPOSITION NO

This Book Belongs To:

_____

Need more Composition Notebooks - college ruled or wide ruled?
Just go straight to our Amazon page at ImagineNotebooks.com!

Need more Quad Ruled 5x5 or 4x4 Graph Notebooks?
Just go straight to our Amazon page at ImagineGraphbooks.com!

IMAGINE NOTEBOOKS
QUALITY NOTEBOOKS WITH DESIGNER COVERS

WIDE RULED
COMPOSITION NOTEBOOK

Need more Composition Notebooks - college ruled or wide ruled?
Just go straight to our Amazon page at ImagineNotebooks.com!

Need more Quad Ruled 5x5 or 4x4 Graph Notebooks?
Just go straight to our Amazon page at ImagineGraphbooks.com!

IMAGINE NOTEBOOKS
QUALITY NOTEBOOKS WITH DESIGNER COVERS

Made in the USA
Las Vegas, NV
08 December 2024